The House of a Mouse

The House of a Mouse

Poems by
AILEEN FISHER

illustrated by
JOAN SANDIN

A Charlotte Zolotow Book

Harper & Row, Publishers

Library of Congress Cataloging-in-Publication Data
Fisher, Aileen Lucia, 1906–
    The house of a mouse : poems / by Aileen Fisher ; illustrated by
Joan Sandin. — 1st ed.
        p.   cm.
    "A Charlotte Zolotow book."
    Summary: A collection of poems about mice, what they eat, where
they live, and how they look.
    ISBN 0-06-021848-7 : $
    ISBN 0-06-021849-5 (lib. bdg.) : $
    1. Mice—Juvenile poetry.   2. Children's poetry, American.
    [1. Mice—Poetry.   2. American poetry.]   I. Sandin, Joan, ill.
    II. Title.
PS3511.I7294H65   1988
811'.54—dc19   87-24947
                                                                      CIP
                                                                      AC

Other Books by **Aileen Fisher**

Portrait

Such big eyes
for one so small,
such big ears
to hear-it-all,

Such trim feet
in barefoot shoes,
such long whiskers
full of news,

Such soft fur
to dress you up,
posing near
a buttercup...

That's *you*, little Mouse!

House
Guest

There was a Mouse
whose coat was trim,
whose ears were pink,
whose feet were slim....
It was a timid little Mouse
who slipped inside a lady's house.

The lady saw him.
"H-E-L-P!" she cried.
You'd think a *lion*
had barged inside.
You'd think a *bear* had broken in
instead of just a Mousikin.

Timid as a Mouse?

Who says a Mouse is timid?
"Timid as a mouse."
I think a Mouse is brave at night
to venture from his house
and hunt for things to nibble
and grass and twigs to chew,
when eyes are on the watch for him
the whole night through....

Eyes of owls and cats and skunks,
to mention just a few,
watching for a little Mouse
the whole night through.

*Careful,
Mouse!*

The great horned owl
and the gray-eared cat
look something alike.
Have you thought of that?
　　And they both catch Mice.

With ear tufts up
and with round, sharp eyes,
the great horned owl
is a big-cat size.
    And they both catch Mice.

But the owl's sharp beak
and the cat's flat nose
are very unlike,
as are their toes.
    But they both catch Mice!

Mouseways

Hidden away
under the hay
out of the sun,
Meadow Mice run.

Sharp little teeth
cut roads beneath
gold hay and green,
narrow, unseen.

Quick little feet
know every street,
but where the streets go
we never know.

Deer
Mouse

Who tells the little Deer Mouse
when summer goes away
that she should fix a cozy place,
a comfy place to stay,
and fill her cupboard shelves with seeds
from berries, weeds, and hay?

Who tells the little Deer Mouse
before the year is old
that she should wear a warmer coat
to shield her from the cold?

I'm glad that SOMEONE tells her
and she does as she is told.

Pockets

How do you carry
those mini-sized seeds
you gather from grasses
and autumn-brown weeds
to store in your cupboard
for cold-weather needs,
little Mouse?

I know! You have pockets
without any leaks
for toting home seeds
that will last you for weeks.
And where are your pockets?
Inside of your cheeks,
little Mouse!

First
Snow

When autumn stills
the crickets
and yellow leaves turn brown,
I wonder what
a Mouseling thinks
as snow starts falling down,
and petal
after petal
goes trickling down his nose
and there's
a strange, cold tickle
between his slender toes?

17

First Snowfall

The little Mouse
in her knothole house,
where her bed is warm and dry...
does she get a shock
when it's snow o'clock
and whiteness fills the sky?

She only knows
about grass that grows,
and weed stalks turned to gold.
She never has heard
a single word
about the snow and cold.

On a sudden night
when the world turns white
and green and gold are through,
the little Mouse
in her knothole house...
does she wonder what to do?

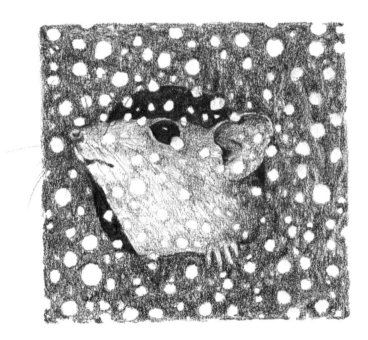

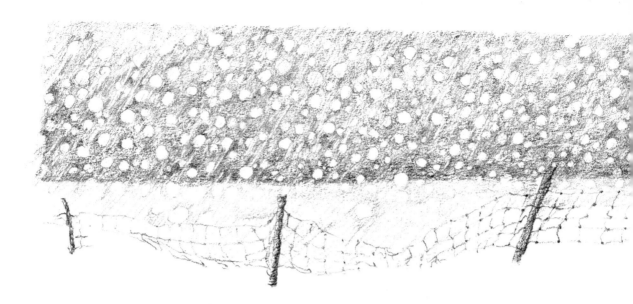

When It's Snowing

Little Mouse, with narrow feet
that you keep so white and neat,
when it's snowing, freezing, blowing,
do you get enough to eat?

You're too little, Mouse, to stray
from your house on such a day.
Weren't you wise to gather scores
of munchy seeds to eat indoors!

Under
the
Snow

Do you know, do you know
where little Mice go
when the meadow is white
with billows of snow?

They dive out of sight
and nibble and play
in tunnels of white
all hidden away...
and if they play "snowballs"
I really can't say.

A Cozy Little House

Do you know where a Mouse
built a cozy little house
when summer had gone by?

Not in a hole,
like a scratchy little mole,
but under the hazy sky.

A nest like a muff
made of cattail fluff
on a cattail that was dry...

That's where a Mouse
built a cozy little house,
and that's where so would I.

Winter
Nests

I wonder if the bluebirds know
in the southland where they go
that now the weeds wear fluffy caps
and hills have covers on their laps
and all the nests are full of snow
except the one that makes a house
for little Mrs. Whitefoot Mouse?

Christmas
Mouse

On the soft white snow
there's a thin white track
where a little Mouse ran
but didn't come back…
for close to some rocks
where the tall weeds lean
the little Mouse changed
to a submarine!

At the foot of a fir
he ducked down under—
does he live in a house
down there, I wonder,
with a wreath on his door
for his friends to see,
and a sprig of spruce
for a Christmas tree?

24

Snow
Stitches

Who's the one
in winter's house
who likes to stitch and sew?

Around the meadow's
new white blouse
some dainty footprints go.

No, not a hare.
No, not a grouse.
But just a plucky little Mouse...

That's the one
whose footprints show
like stitches in the new white snow.

25

The
House
of a
Mouse

The tiny world of Meadow Mice
can't be very safe and nice

When nibbly sheep and crunchy cows
make earthquake-trembles as they browse,

And horses plunk a giant hoof
beside (or on) a Mouse's roof.

I'm glad *my* house is stronger far
than Mouses' houses ever are.

A Mouse and Her House

A Mouse has a house
but she doesn't keep it tidy.

She doesn't use a mop
from Friday to Friday.

She doesn't sweep her room
with a broom on Monday
or Tuesday or Wednesday
or right through Sunday.

But a Mouse in a blouse
of velveteen is tidy
when it comes to *herself*
from Friday to Friday:

She washes her hands,
her fingers, her toes,
her ears and her whiskers,
her tail and her nose.

She washes the fur
of her velvety clothes
not only on Friday,
but Thursday and Sunday
and Tuesday and Wednesday
and Saturday and Monday.

Surprise

I wonder…
does Mrs. Meadow Mouse
dust off her jacket
and smooth her blouse
and ask her neighbors
to stop their labors
and hurry to see
her big surprise—

Six little babies
with tight-shut eyes,
curling together
(as Mouselings do),
rosy and dozy
and squeaky new?

30

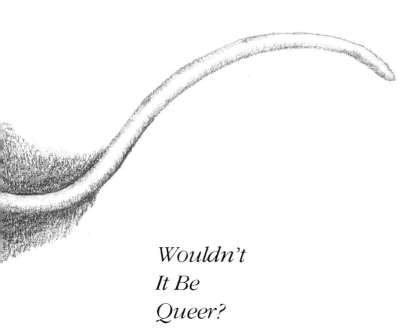

Wouldn't It Be Queer?

"Come and eat your dish of seeds,
Come and drink your dew.
Try these green and tender weeds—
they are good for you.

"Brush away the crumbs you find,
comb your whiskers nice...."
Wouldn't it be queer to mind
parents who were MICE?

SAINT ★ SEIYA
KNIGHTS
OF THE
ZODIAC
™

Vol. 11
To You I Entrust Athena
Story & Art by **Masami Kurumada**

DRAGON
SHIRYÛ

PHOENIX IKKI

PEGASUS
SEIYA

SWAN
HYÔGA

ANDROMEDA
SHUN

MIRO

SHURA

CAMUS

APHRODITE

PRINCESS SIENNA

YEARS AGO, THE GOLD KNIGHT AIORIOS ENTRUSTED LORD NOBU OF THE GRANDE FOUNDATION WITH THE INFANT PRINCESS SIENNA, THE INCARNATION OF THE GODDESS ATHENA. TO RAISE WARRIORS WITH THE STRENGTH TO FIGHT FOR ATHENA, LORD NOBU SENT HIS OWN 100 CHILDREN OUT INTO THE WORLD TO TRAIN AS KNIGHTS. THE FOUR BRONZE KNIGHTS, SEIYA, HYÔGA, SHIRYÛ AND SHUN, HAVING SUCCEEDED BRILLIANTLY IN THEIR TRAINING, ACCOMPANY PRINCESS SIENNA TO SANCTUARY, HEADQUARTERS OF KNIGHTHOOD. BUT PRINCESS SIENNA IS WOUNDED AT THE GATES OF SANCTUARY, FORCING THE BRONZE KNIGHTS TO FIGHT THEIR WAY TO THE ONLY PERSON WHO CAN HELP HER : THE MYSTERIOUS MASTER OF SANCTUARY.

JUST AS SEIYA AND HIS FRIENDS ARE ABOUT TO FALL BEFORE THE ATTACK OF THE GOLD KNIGHT, SHAKA, IKKI, THE REBELLIOUS PHOENIX KNIGHT, SHOWS UP TO HELP THEM. BY ELEVATING HIS COSMO, IKKI IS ABLE TO MATCH SHAKA'S GODLIKE STRENGTH, AND HE AND SHAKA GO TO THEIR DEATHS TOGETHER. NOW HYÔGA FACES MIRO, THE SCORPION KNIGHT. CAN HYÔGA DEFLECT MIRO'S CRIMSON NEEDLES?

THE STORY THUS FAR

ooo

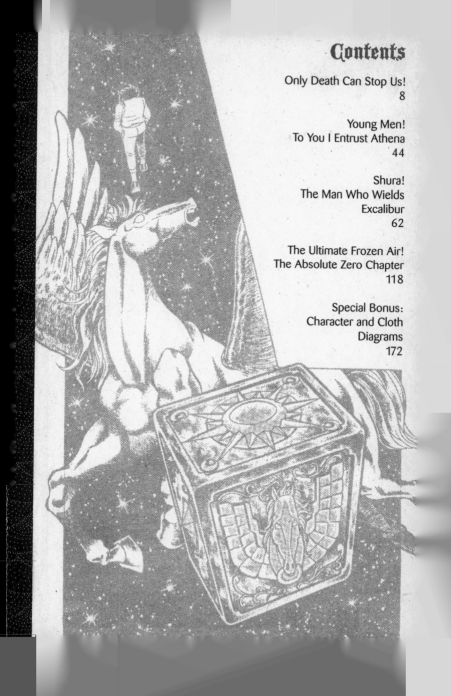

Contents

SORRY, HYÔGA, BUT USING YOUR FROZEN TORNADO AFTER BEING STUNG BY THE SCARLET NEEDLE WAS FUTILE...

JUST LOOK AT YOURSELF!

WHAT!?

NO! WHAT THE--!?

THE TINY WOUNDS INFLICTED BY THE SCARLET NEEDLE HAVE ENLARGED AND ARE GUSHING BLOOD!!

UNH...I'M LOSING FEELING IN MY LIMBS... MY VISION IS GROWING DIM...

EVEN MY SKIN AND MY TONGUE FEEL STRANGE! WHAT'S HAPPENING TO ME?

MY HEARING IS STARTING TO GO, TOO...

10

THE MORE YOU BLEED, THE MORE YOUR SENSES WILL FADE.

THE VENOM OF THE SCARLET NEEDLE IS DESTROYING YOUR SENSES!

WHAT!?

MIRO...I-I HAVE TO TAKE YOU DOWN...

UNH... THEN... BEFORE THEY GO COMPLETELY...

ARGH!!

CAN'T YOU SEE THAT YOUR ATTACKS HAVE NO EFFECT?

IT'S HOPELESS!

FOOL! HAVEN'T YOU GUESSED CAMUS' TRUE PURPOSE?

WHAT!?

THOUGH YOU WERE IN A NEAR-DEATH STATE, AFTER MANY EONS, YOU MIGHT'VE BEEN RE-SUSCITATED.

CAMUS CONFRONTED YOU AT THE PALACE OF THE SCALES AND SEALED YOU IN THAT COFFIN OF ICE TO SPARE YOUR LIFE!

C-CAMUS...

WITH THAT HOPE, CAMUS REMOVED YOU FROM THE BATTLE ...

EASTERN SIBERIA SIX YEARS AGO

SO YOU'RE THE LAD WHO CAME ALL THE WAY FROM JAPAN TO BE A KNIGHT...

YES.

NOW THE SEA ABOVE THE SHIP IS FROZEN SOLID, AND MAMA IS TRAPPED FOREVER AT THE BOTTOM OF THE COLD SIBERIAN SEA.

I WANT THE STRENGTH TO GET HER OUT...

WHY DO YOU WANT TO BECOME A KNIGHT, BOY?

DO YOU WANT TO BE STRONG?

LAST YEAR, MY MOTHER DIED IN A SHIPWRECK.

14

THAT'S WHY YOU WANT TO BE A KNIGHT?

Y-YES.

WITH SUCH CHILDISH IDEAS IN YOUR HEAD, EVEN IF YOU BECAME A KNIGHT, YOU'D SOON BE KILLED.

THEN YOU WILL SURELY DIE.

WHAT?

LOOK OVER THERE, HYŌGA.

THEY HAVE SURVIVED THE ASSAULT OF THE SUN FOR AGES!

TO BE A KNIGHT, YOU MUST BECOME STRONG LIKE THOSE PERMANENT ICE RIDGES!

THOSE MOUNTAINS ARE PERMANENT ICE RIDGES. THEY HAVE SUCH ENDURING STRENGTH THAT THEY HAVE SURVIVED FOR TENS OF THOUSANDS OF YEARS.

LEARN THE MEANING OF TRUE STRENGTH FROM THE ICE RIDGES OF SIBERIA, HYŌGA!

I...I WILL.

REMEMBER THIS--HOWEVER STRONG THE ENEMY YOU FACE, ALWAYS REMAIN CALM!

15

N-NO...

YOUR SENSES WILL RETURN IN A FEW DAYS.

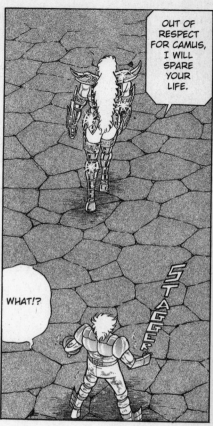

OUT OF RESPECT FOR CAMUS, I WILL SPARE YOUR LIFE.

HMM?

YOU'RE JUST LIKE CAMUS, MIRO-- BUT THIS ISN'T WHAT I WANT...

WHAT!?

STAGGER

EVEN IF I EMERGED ALIVE FROM THAT COFFIN OF ICE DECADES OR CENTURIES FROM NOW, WHAT VALUE WOULD MY LIFE HAVE?

HOW CAN I SLEEP WHILE MY BROTHERS ARE FIGHTING AND SUFFERING?

EVEN DEPRIVED OF ALL MY SENSES, I'LL FIGHT ON AS LONG AS LIFE REMAINS IN ME!

HE'D RATHER DIE AS A TRUE KNIGHT THAN LIVE BY OUR MERCY!

DID YOU HEAR THAT, CAMUS?

THE IDEA OF SPARING HIS LIFE IS AN INSULT TO THIS ONE!

GUARDIAN OF THE PALACE OF THE JEWELED URN, DID YOU HEAR HYŌGA'S WORDS?

18

THANK YOU FOR RECOGNIZING HYÔGA'S KNIGHTHOOD.

MIRO...

THEN I WILL STRIKE THE FATAL BLOW WITH ALL MY MIGHT!

I ACKNOWLEDE HYÔGA AS A TRUE KNIGHT!

YOU HEAR ME, CAMUS!?

...FOR ATHENA, FOR YOUR FRIENDS... WELL DONE, BRAVE HYÔGA!

MY DEAR HYÔGA, YOU INTEND TO GO ON, EVEN IF IT MEANS YOUR DEATH...

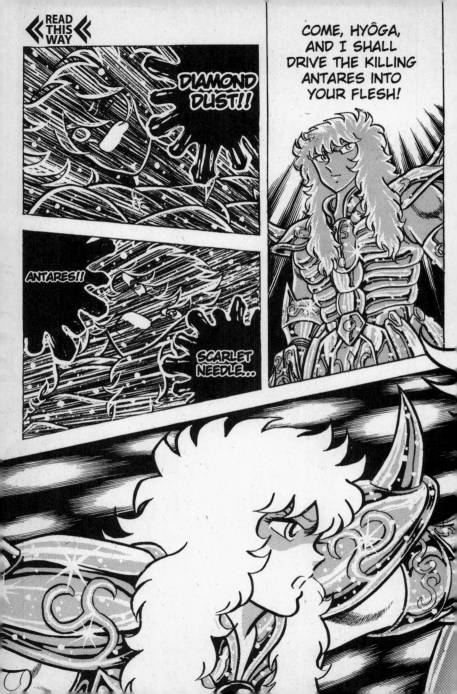

HUH?

AH!

HYÔGA!!

NOW...

IT WAS YOUR WISH TO DIE IN A FAIR BATTLE, HYÔGA.

WHAT!?

HE'S BEEN GONE A LONG TIME. WHAT IS HE DOING?

JAB, HASN'T GEKI RETURNED FROM HIS ERRAND?

THE FLAME OF THE PALACE OF THE SCORPION HAS GONE OUT. THERE ARE ONLY FOUR HOURS LEFT!

I WONDER IF SEIYA AND THE OTHERS HAVE MADE IT TO THE PALACE OF THE CENTAUR YET...

PRINCESS SIENNA'S BELOVED GOLDEN STAFF, AND...

WHAT COULD HE BE RETRIEVING FROM THE JET IN THE ARENA?

WHAT!? YOU BROUGHT **THAT** ALL THE WAY FROM JAPAN!?

IT MUST'VE BEEN IN OUR LAST EXCHANGE OF BLOWS...

BUT... BUT WHEN?

ANTARES!!

SCARLET NEEDLE...

DIAMOND DUST!!

UNH... THE DIAMOND DUST'S FRIGID AIR HAS FROZEN EVEN MY GOLD CLOTH!

IF I HADN'T BEEN WEARING A GOLD CLOTH, I WOULD HAVE FALLEN FIRST.

...THE DIAMOND DUST STRUCK MY 15 STAR LIFE POINTS!!

HYÔGA, AS I STRUCK WITH ANTARES...

...I HAVE LOST THIS FIGHT.

I HAVE WON THE BATTLE BETWEEN LIFE AND DEATH, BUT...

IN THE LAST INSTANT BEFORE HE FELL, HYÔGA ELEVATED HIS COSMO HIGHER THAN MY OWN!!

KLANK! KLANK!

WH-WHAT?

WHERE ARE YOU TRYING TO GO, HYÔGA?

EVEN UNCONSCIOUS...

YET YOU MAKE NO ATTEMPT TO SAVE YOURSELF...

...BUT TRY TO FULFILL YOUR MISSION INSTEAD...

BUT YOU LACK THE STRENGTH. TOO MUCH BLOOD HAS SPILLED FROM THE WOUNDS OF THE SCARLET NEEDLE. ONLY A FEW MINUTES OF LIFE REMAIN.

OR IS IT TO THE MASTER, WHOM YOU BELIEVE TO BE EVIL?

TO YOUR BROTHERS? TO CAMUS?

KLANK

KLAK

KLAK

KLAK

THE BLEEDING WILL STOP, AND YOUR SENSES WILL SOON RETURN.

UNH...

BUT... WHY?

I JUST STRUCK THE TRUE CENTER POINT, THE VITAL POINT THAT STOPS BLOOD LOSS.

...JUST HOW FAR YOU BRONZES CAN GO. AND HOW THIS BATTLE WILL END...

HEH. I WANT TO SEE...

CAN YOU HEAR ME, HYÔGA?

THE GOLD SAGITTARIUS CLOTH!!

WHAT!?

SHUT UP! WE DIDN'T BRING IT FOR THE BATTLES!!

THE PRINCESS BROUGHT THE SAGITTARIUS CLOTH HERE TO RETURN IT TO ITS TRUE OWNER.

WHY DIDN'T YOU BRING IT OUT SOONER!?

WHAT? I THOUGHT YOU LEFT IT BACK AT LORD NOBU'S MANOR IN JAPAN!

SEIYA COULD'VE USED IT IN HIS BATTLES WITH THE GOLD KNIGHTS!!

D-DON'T TELL ME...

WHO'S THAT!?

TRUE OWNER!?

34

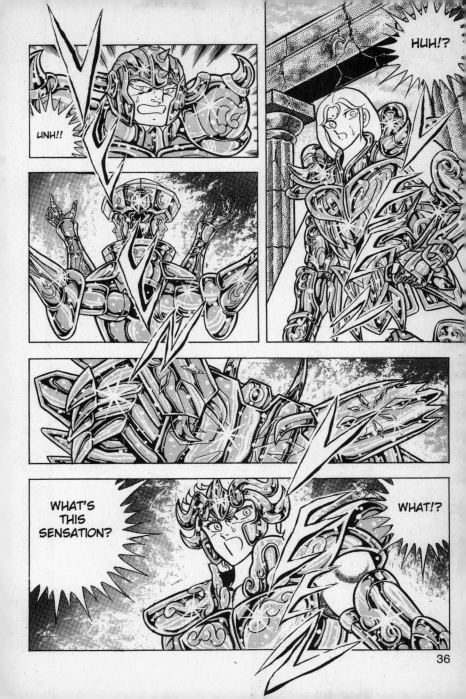

IM-
POSSIBLE
!!

HAH! THE GOLD CLOTHS ARE RESONATING, AS THOUGH CALLING TO EACH OTHER!!

DOES THIS MEAN THAT THE SAGITTARIUS CLOTH HAS RETURNED TO SANCTUARY AFTER 13 YEARS!?

THIS MEANS THAT ALL OF THE GOLD CLOTHS HAVE GATHERED IN ONE PLACE!

WHOOSH

SHIRYÛ! WHAT'S THAT?

A SHOOTING STAR?

IT WENT INTO THE PALACE OF THE CENTAUR!!

WHAT!?

THIS IS THE NINTH PALACE, THE PALACE OF THE CENTAUR. IT WAS AIORIOS' PALACE.

THIS ALL BEGAN WHEN AIOROS RESCUED PRINCESS SIENNA--OR RATHER, ATHENA--13 YEARS AGO...

WHOA! WAIT, SEIYA!

WELL, WE CAN'T STAND HERE PONDERING. TIME'S RUNNING OUT. WE HAVE TO HURRY TO THE NEXT PALACE, SEIYA.

YEAH, THERE'S NO ONE HERE TO STOP US, SO WE CAN PASS RIGHT THROUGH.

THAT'S--

WHAT!?

THE GOLD SAGITTARIUS CLOTH!!

SO THAT WAS THE SHOOTING STAR WE SAW JUST NOW...

PRINCESS SIENNA MUST HAVE BROUGHT IT WITH HER, BUT--

BUT WHAT'S IT DOING HERE? IT'S SUPPOSED TO BE SAFE IN JAPAN.

46

THEY'RE GREEK LETTERS...

WORDS... CARVED IN THE WALL UNDER THE SHATTERED VENEER. .

WHAT!?

IT SEEMS TO BE AIOROS' FINAL TESTAMENT.

THE SAGITTARIUS CLOTH WASN'T AIMING AT SEIYA.

HYÔGA!

IT WAS TRYING TO SHOW US THIS TESTAMENT.

THANK THE GODS YOU MADE IT THROUGH THE PALACE OF THE SCORPION!!

"...AIOROS."

"...I ENTRUST ATHENA TO YOUR CARE."

"YOU YOUTHS WHO HAVE COME TO THIS PLACE..."

I ENTRUST ATHENA TO YOUR CARE...

AIOROS WAS WAITING FOR US, ALL THIS TIME...

SOME POWER IS RESTORING MY STRENGTH...

WHAT'S THIS FEELING WELLING UP FROM THE BOTTOM OF MY SOUL?

TEARS... I DON'T UNDER-STAND...

...IN THE PALACE OF THE CENTAUR, NOT KNOWING WHEN WE MIGHT ARRIVE...OR IF WE EVER WOULD...

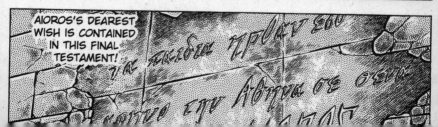

AIOROS'S DEAREST WISH IS CONTAINED IN THIS FINAL TESTAMENT!

AIOROS IS ENTRUSTING ATHENA TO US.

THERE'S AN OLD CHINESE PROVERB THAT RÔSHI TAUGHT ME...ABOUT ENTRUSTING ONE'S CHILD TO ANOTHER LIKE AN HEIRLOOM.

HE HAS ENTRUSTED US WITH THE MOST PRECIOUS THING OF ALL.

WHEN HE DIES, A MAN WILL ONLY ENTRUST HIS CHILD TO ONE WHO IS TRUE!

HE HAS ACKNOWL-EDGED US AS TRUE MEN.

AIOROS, RIGHT HERE, RIGHT NOW, WE VOW TO YOU ANEW-- WE WILL DEFEND ATHENA!!

AND WE ONLY HAVE THREE HOURS LEFT!

ONLY THREE PALACES STAND BETWEEN US AND THE MASTER'S CHAMBER!

...AND SAVE ATHENA'S LIFE.

IF ANY ONE OF US SURVIVES, HE MUST DRAG THE MASTER OUT...

I'M GRATEFUL TO ALL OF YOU!

IT'S A MIRACLE WE'VE MANAGED TO GET THIS FAR.

WE'RE HERE BECAUSE WE ALL GAVE OUR UTMOST!

WE ALL FEEL THE SAME WAY. IT WOULD'VE BEEN IMPOSSIBLE FOR ANY ONE OF US TO MAKE IT THIS FAR ON HIS OWN.

54

THE 10TH PALACE STANDS BEFORE US-- THE PALACE OF THE ROCK GOAT!

LET'S GO!

THE SUN'S GONE DOWN!!

THERE ARE ONLY THREE FLAMES LEFT ON THE FIRE CLOCK!

MAYBE WE CAN PASS RIGHT THROUGH!

I DON'T SENSE ANY COSMO!

NO, DON'T LET YOUR GUARD DOWN!

AAAH!!

ARE YOU ALL RIGHT, SHUN!?

S-SEIYA... I'M SORRY...

WHAT!?

AH! SHIRYÛ!!

SHIRYÛ'S STRANDED AT THE PALACE OF THE ROCK GOAT!!

OH NO!

OR DID THE CHASM I CREATED MAKE YOU WEAK-KNEED?

KRUNCH

IF I HAD LEAPT, TOO, WE MIGHT'VE ALL BEEN HURLED INTO THE DEPTHS OF THE EARTH BY YOUR SECOND ATTACK.

HEH HEH HEH... YOU TOLD YOUR COMRADES TO JUMP, BUT YOU APPARENTLY LACKED THE COURAGE TO DO IT YOURSELF.

HA! YOU MEAN YOU STAYED BEHIND SO THAT THOSE THREE COULD SAFELY ESCAPE, YOU IMPUDENT FOOL!?

YOU'RE GOING TO REGRET THAT DECISION, BOY!!

NOW I'M REALLY GLAD I DIDN'T JUMP!

WHAT?

I'LL BATTER YOU WITH EVERY OUNCE OF STRENGTH LEFT IN MY COSMO AND AVENGE AIOROS!!

SHIRYÛ!!

IF WE STAY HERE, SHIRYÛ'S SACRIFICE WILL HAVE BEEN FOR NOTHING.

COME ON, YOU TWO.

SHIRYÛ!!

SHIRYÛ, THIS IS NOT GOODBYE!!

A-ALL RIGHT, WE'LL GO ON...

RIGHT...

64

SHURA'S ARM IS LIKE A RAZOR-SHARP BLADE!

UNH...THAT'S THE PUNCH OF A MAN WHO CAN SPLIT THE EARTH...

NO, IT'S MORE LIKE THE SLASH OF A SWORD...

MY ARM IS CALLED EXCALIBUR, AND NOTHING CAN STAND BEFORE IT!!

HEH HEH HEH... DID YOU JUST REALIZE THAT, BOY? ALL OF MY LIMBS ARE LIKE HONED STEEL! I AM THE STRONGEST OF THE 12 GOLD KNIGHTS!

UGH!

HOW NAIVE! YOU'VE USED A CHILD'S MOVE AGAINST ME!

YOU SEE? YOU'VE BEEN SENT FLYING BY THE FORCE OF YOUR OWN ATTACK!

WHAT !?

69

I'LL LOP OFF YOUR HEAD AND PUT YOU TO REST!

UNH...

UGH!

72

UNH...

HMPH!

K RRAK

HE SLICED THROUGH THE MIGHTY DRAGON SHIELD!

WHOA!

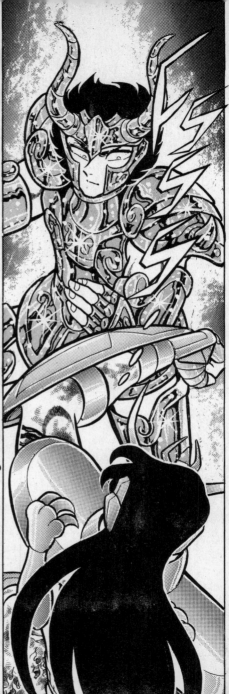

SHURA'S ARM REALLY IS THE ALL-SLICING EXCALIBUR! I'M NO MATCH FOR IT...

OTHERS HAVE BEEN STRONG ENOUGH TO DESTROY A CLOTH, BUT NO ONE EVER SLICED ONE APART WITH SUCH EASE...

UNH...HE CUT THE DRAGON CLOTH TO PIECES...

THIS TIME, IT'S NOT YOUR CLOTH, BUT **YOU** I WILL SLICE IN TWO!!

HAVE YOU ACCEPTED YOUR DOOM, SHIRYÛ?

A-A DREAM ...?

WHUP

OH!

HOW HORRIBLE-- I DREAMED THAT SHIRYÛ HAD BEEN CUT IN TWO...

SHIRYÛ, PLEASE COME HOME SOON...

N-NO...I CAN'T GO BACK TO SLEEP...

I FORBID IT...

...YOU MUST NOT DIE...

SHIRYÛ...

YOU STILL HAVE THE STRENGTH TO STAND...AND EVEN BLOCK MY BLOW WITH YOUR BARE HANDS! BUT HOW?

SHURA, ITS A MOVE THAT WILL DEFEAT YOU!!

THE ULTIMATE SECRET MOVE OF BŪDO, PASSED DOWN IN MY HOMELAND OF JAPAN...

SHINKEN-SHIRAHA-DORI!*

WH-WHAT?

*BARE-HANDED SWORD CATCH

ARGH!!

HOW CAN SO MUCH STRENGTH BE LEFT IN HIM!?

IM-POSSIBLE!

WHAT'S THIS!?

UNH...

78

NOW A MIGHTY COSMO ENERGIZES HIS BODY...

THE RISING DRAGON APPEARED ON SHIRYÛ'S BACK...

IT'S AS IF A DRAGON GOD HAS POSSESSED SHIRYÛ!

ITS POWER SURPASSES EVEN MY OWN...

HAS SHIRYÛ UNKNOWINGLY AWAKENED TO THE SEVENTH SENSE!?

I'VE KNOWN ABOUT THE RISING DRAGON BLOW'S FLAW SINCE THE TIME SEIYA NOTICED IT...

SH-SHIRYÛ, YOU...

UNH...

TH-THEN YOU INTENTIONALLY EXPOSED IT TO ME...

...IN ORDER TO TRAP ME...

LIE STILL. MY BLOW DAMAGED YOUR HEART.

ANYWAY, WHAT WOULD YOU DO IF YOU GOT TO YOUR FEET?

IF YOU MOVE, YOUR HEART MAY BURST.

YOU DISABLED MY LEFT ARM, BUT I STILL HAVE MY SWORD-EDGE RIGHT ARM AND BOTH MY LEGS!

YOUR HEART CAN'T WITHSTAND ANOTHER BLOW. IF YOU UNLEASH THE RISING DRAGON AGAIN, YOU'RE A DEAD MAN!

YOU'RE FINISHED, SHIRYÛ!!

89

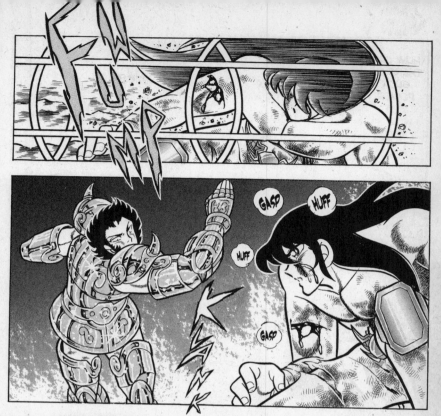

I-I TOLD YOU THAT IF YOU DESTROYED ME, I'D TAKE YOU DOWN WITH ME, SHURA...

IT'S PAINFUL TO WATCH A MAN OF YOUR CALIBER THROW AWAY HIS LIFE SO FOOLISHLY!

DEPRIVED OF YOUR GREATEST ATTACK, YOU HAVE NOTHING LEFT.

WHAT!?

HOW CAN THERE BE SUCH POWER LEFT WITHIN HIM?

HE STANDS AT THE BRINK OF DEATH, AND YET THIS MAN'S COSMO, INSTEAD OF DWINDLING, GROWS STRONGER...

FORGIVE ME, RÔSHI... I HAVE TO BREAK YOUR PROHIBITION...

WHAT'S THIS!?

SEAL IT AWAY WITHIN YOU FOREVER!

SHIRYŪ, THE ASCENDANT DRAGON BLOW IS A FORBIDDEN MOVE.

THERE IS A SAYING: "THE ASCENDANT DRAGON HAS REGRETS." THIS MEANS THAT, WHEN ONE ATTAINS THE PINNACLE OF LIFE, THE ONLY PATH REMAINING LEADS TO RUIN.

AN ASCENDANT DRAGON IS ONE THAT HAS SOARED TO THE ZENITH OF THE HEAVENS.

A FORBIDDEN MOVE? I CAN NEVER USE THE ASCENDANT DRAGON BLOW?

THE ASCENDANT DRAGON BLOW IS AN UNPARALLELED MOVE.

CORRECT!

YOU HAVE MASTERED THE RISING DRAGON BLOW, AND YOU HAVE EVEN LEARNED HOW TO SUBLIMATE IT INTO THE ASCENDANT DRAGON BLOW.

DO YOU UNDERSTAND, SHIRYÛ? SEAL AWAY THE ASCENDANT DRAGON BLOW AND NEVER USE IT...

THERE EXISTS NOT ONE HUMAN WHO COULD WITHSTAND IT, NOT EVEN MYSELF...

BY MASTERING IT, IT WOULD NOT BE AN EXAGGERATION TO SAY THAT YOU HAVE BECOME INVINCIBLE ON THIS EARTH.

UNFORTUNATELY, YOUR OWN FLESH COULD NOT WITHSTAND ITS POWER.

INCREDIBLE!

BUT TRUE, NONETHELESS. THAT IS HOW GREAT ITS POWER IS.

IF YOU USE IT, YOU WILL SURELY DIE!!

THE ASCENDANT DRAGON BLOW IS A SWORD THAT CUTS BOTH WAYS. IT DESTROYS ANY ENEMY, NO MATTER HOW STRONG, AT THE PRICE OF THE USER'S LIFE...

UNH...

WHU

KRA

WH-WHAT THE...? SHIRYÛ, WHAT DO YOU HAVE THAT MAKES ME TREMBLE WITH FEAR!?

I'M NOT SURE WHAT WILL HAPPEN IF I USE THIS MOVE...

...BUT I KNOW ONE THING!

THE ONE MOVE THAT MY BELOVED MASTER RÔSHI FORBADE ME TO USE...

WH-WHAT? LIBRA RÔSHI?

UNH!

HUH?

OH!

THE CAPRICORN FLAME HAS GONE OUT!!

THERE'S THE ELEVENTH PALACE, THE PALACE OF THE JEWELED URN!!

WHOSE COSMO IS THAT!?

IF WE KEEP HURTLING UPWARD LIKE THIS, THE AIR FRICTION WILL BURN US TO SPACE DUST.

D-DO YOU UNDERSTAND WHAT YOU'RE DOING?

SINCE YOU HAVE NO CLOTH, YOU WILL DIE FIRST, SHIRYÛ.

BUT I'M WEARING A GOLD CLOTH, SO I'LL SURVIVE LONGER THAN YOU WILL.

WHAT? YOU WANT TO WIN THAT BADLY?

I WAS PREPARED TO DIE FROM THE VERY BEGINNING. I TOLD YOU I'D TAKE YOU ALONG NO MATTER WHAT...

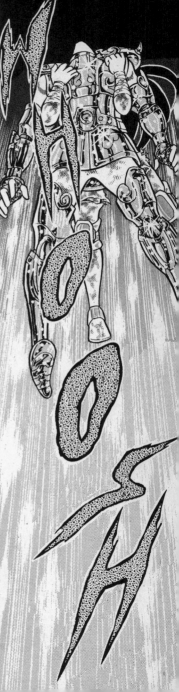

I NEVER IMAGINED A MAN LIKE YOU COULD EXIST IN THIS WORLD, SHIRYÛ.

THAT'S INSANE! I CAN'T BELIEVE IT!

SHIRYÛ, YOU MUST NOT DIE...

I BELIEVED THAT ALL HUMAN BEINGS FIGHT ONLY FOR THEM-SELVES.

I THOUGHT YOU PUT YOUR LIFE ON THE LINE PURELY FOR PERSONAL GLORY.

A MAN LIKE YOU MUST LIVE TO FIGHT FOR ATHENA...

I BELIEVED THAT THOSE WHO HAD POWER, THOSE WHO WERE VICTORIOUS, WERE QUALIFIED TO DECLARE THEMSELVES JUST.

THAT'S WHY I THOUGHT THAT EVEN IF THE MASTER WERE EVIL, IF HE PUSHED THROUGH WITH POWER, HE MIGHT DO SOME GOOD.

SHURA...

I AM UNWORTHY TO BE A KNIGHT, MUCH LESS A GOLD KNIGHT...

NOW I SEE THAT I WAS MISTAKEN.

110

SHIRYÛ!!

UNH!

I'M SORRY, BUT WE DON'T HAVE TIME TO MOURN OUR BROTHER'S DEATH.

HUH?

CAMUS, GUARDIAN OF THE PALACE OF THE JEWELED URN.

HE'S HYŌGA'S MASTER, THE ONE WHO IMPRISONED HIM IN THE FREEZING COFFIN BACK AT THE PALACE OF THE SCALES!

113

HYÔGA
...

SEIYA, SHUN, GO ON AHEAD!

I WANT NO INTERFERENCE FROM ANYONE, NOT EVEN YOU!!

LEAVE MY MASTER TO ME!!

HYOGA...

NO, I WILL SAY NOTHING.

HYÔGA... I...

MASTER CAMUS...

THANK YOU!

FOR TEACHING ME TO BE A KNIGHT IN THE WASTES OF EASTERN SIBERIA, WORDS OF THANKS ARE NOT ENOUGH...

...SO I'LL EXPRESS MY GRATITUDE IN THE LANGUAGE OF A KNIGHT—THROUGH ACTION!

COME, HYÔGA!!

I WILL COMBINE EVERYTHING YOU'VE TAUGHT ME...

...AND TAKE YOU DOWN, MASTER CAMUS!

VERY WELL, IN THAT CASE, I'LL ALSO BRING EVERYTHING INTO PLAY AGAINST YOU, AND THIS TIME I WILL BURY YOU FOREVER!

116

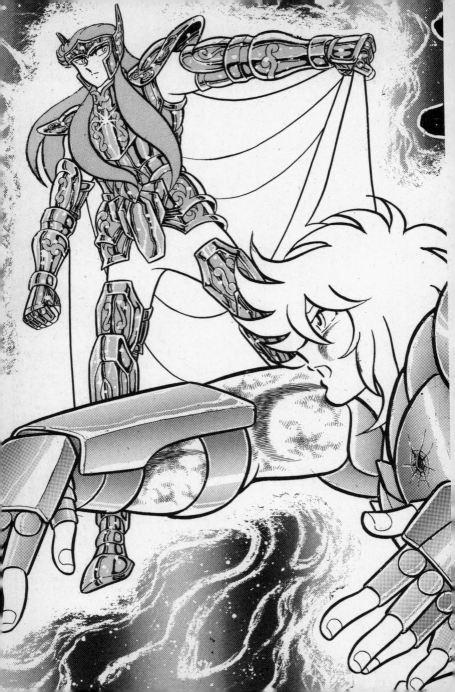

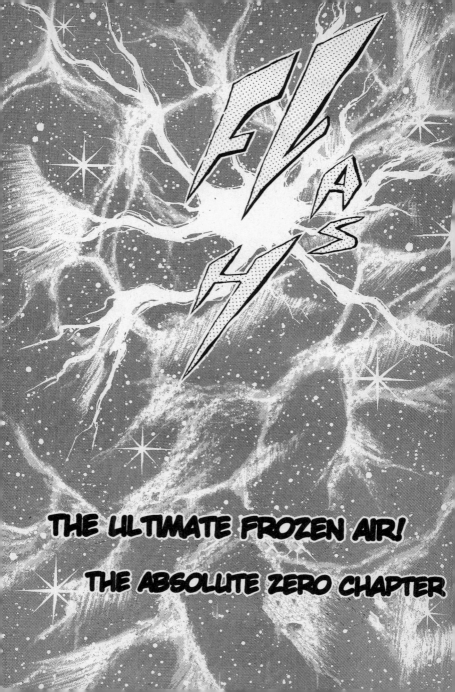

THE ULTIMATE FROZEN AIR!

THE ABSOLUTE ZERO CHAPTER

THEN LET'S TRUST THAT HYŌGA WILL WIN AND PUSH ON!

RIGHT.

OUR GOAL IS THE FINAL PALACE, THE PALACE OF THE TWIN FISH!

LET'S GO, SHUN. HYŌGA DOESN'T WANT US TO INTERFERE.

THOUGH THEY'RE ABOUT TO FACE EACH OTHER IN MORTAL COMBAT, I SENSE SOMETHING ALMOST SACRED BETWEEN HYŌGA AND CAMUS.

ARGH!

M-MY LEG...IT'S FROZEN...

UNH...

UNH... A-ABSOLUTE ZERO...

WHAT IS ABSOLUTE ZERO?

ANSWER, HYŌGA!

HYÔGA, ABSOLUTE ZERO IS THE TEMPERATURE AT WHICH ALL THINGS FREEZE: -459 DEGREES FAHRENHEIT!

EASTERN SIBERIA, 6 YEARS EARLIER...

PUT ANOTHER WAY, IT IS THE TEMPERATURE AT WHICH ALL MOVEMENT CEASES!

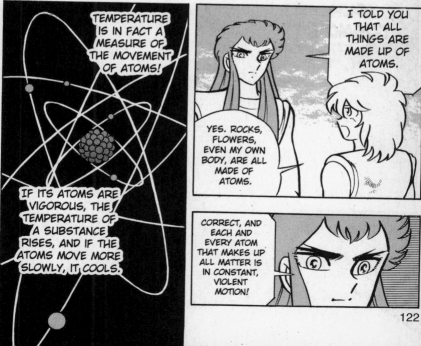

TEMPERATURE IS IN FACT A MEASURE OF THE MOVEMENT OF ATOMS!

IF ITS ATOMS ARE VIGOROUS, THE TEMPERATURE OF A SUBSTANCE RISES, AND IF THE ATOMS MOVE MORE SLOWLY, IT COOLS.

I TOLD YOU THAT ALL THINGS ARE MADE UP OF ATOMS.

YES. ROCKS, FLOWERS, EVEN MY OWN BODY, ARE ALL MADE OF ATOMS.

CORRECT, AND EACH AND EVERY ATOM THAT MAKES UP ALL MATTER IS IN CONSTANT, VIOLENT MOTION!

122

BUT TO MASTER BATTLE MOVES INVOLVING ICE, YOU MUST STOP THE MOTION OF ATOMS, NOT SMASH THEM.

THE FOUNDATION OF DESTRUCTION LIES IN CRUSHING ATOMS.

DO YOU UNDERSTAND, HYÔGA? IF YOU WANT TO FREEZE SOMETHING, YOU NEED ONLY TO IMMOBILIZE ITS ATOMS.

REMEMBER, HYÔGA, YOU MUST STOP THE MOTION OF ATOMS...

...BY THE POWER OF YOUR COSMO!!

WHAT!?

A MOVE THAT A KNIGHT HAS SEEN ONCE WILL NEVER WORK ON HIM AGAIN!

YOU TAUGHT ME THAT YOURSELF...

WHAT?

HYŌGA, YOU JUST SUFFERED THE AURORA EXECUTION! AND YET YOU LIVE?

MASTER!!

AND I WILL TAKE YOU DOWN!!

EVEN IF I CAN'T GET ALL THE WAY TO ABSOLUTE ZERO, CAMUS, I SWEAR I WILL ELEVATE MY FROZEN AIR TO YOUR LEVEL!

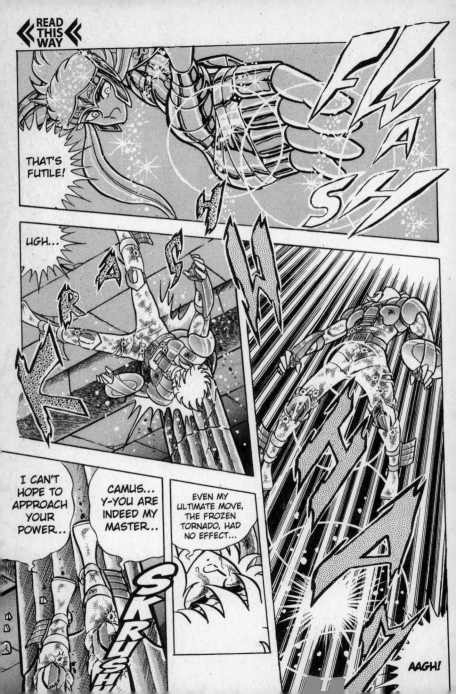

THAT'S FUTILE!

UGH...

I CAN'T HOPE TO APPROACH YOUR POWER...

CAMUS... Y-YOU ARE INDEED MY MASTER...

EVEN MY ULTIMATE MOVE, THE FROZEN TORNADO, HAD NO EFFECT...

AAGH!

AND NOW THERE IS NO ONE TO WIELD LIBRA'S SWORD AND RELEASE YOU. THIS IS THE END FOR YOU, HYÔGA.

NOTHING CAN MELT THE FREEZING COFFIN, AND IT CANNOT BE SHATTERED BY THE COMBINED POWER OF SEVERAL GOLD KNIGHTS.

FWOOSH

DEATH WILL COME VERY SOON, SO WAIT PATIENTLY...

UNH...

CHI...

CHIK

GRRR...

WHAT? HOW CAN...

134

136

IT WOULD HAVE TO BE -459 DEGREES FAHRENHEIT, OR...

TO SHATTER THE FREEZING COFFIN, HIS FROZEN AIR WOULD HAVE TO BE COLDER THAN THAT OF THE FREEZING COFFIN ITSELF...

COULD HYÔGA HAVE SOMEHOW...

...ABSOLUTE ZERO!!

139

THE...

WHAT!?

THE BLASTS OF ICY AIR ARE SWIRLING BETWEEN HYÔGA AND MYSELF!

HYÔGA MUST HAVE UNLEASHED FROZEN AIR EQUAL TO MY OWN!!

141

ALL THINGS HAVE A FREEZING POINT.

UN-FORTUNATELY, YOU STILL CAN'T DEFEAT ME.

IT'S AMAZING THAT YOU WERE ABLE TO ELEVATE YOUR FROZEN AIR TO MY LEVEL!

B-BRILLIANT! WELL DONE, HYŌGA!

CLOTHS ALSO HAVE A FREEZING POINT.

WATER TURNS TO ICE AT 32 DEGREES F, AND ALCOHOL FREEZES AT -174 DEGREES F.

HOWEVER, ONLY A BLAST OF AIR WITH A TEMPERATURE OF -459 DEGREES F CAN FREEZE A GOLD CLOTH!

EVEN SILVER CLOTHS CEASE TO FUNCTION BELOW -330 DEGREES F.

BRONZE CLOTHS FREEZE BELOW -240 DEGREES F! EVEN THOUGH YOUR CLOTH WAS BORN FROM THE PERMANENT ICE WALL, IT IS NO EXCEPTION!

YOU SEE, HYÔGA, AS LONG AS I'M WEARING A GOLD CLOTH, NO MATTER HOW MUCH YOU ELEVATE YOUR FROZEN AIR, YOU'LL NEVER BEAT ME...

YES, IN ORDER TO SHATTER MY GOLD CLOTH, YOU MUST BE ABLE TO GENERATE A BLAST OF ABSOLUTE ZERO!

HYOGA?

THE EFFORT OF MATCHING MY FROZEN AIR HAS MADE HIM PASS OUT...

DON'T FALL ASLEEP! IF YOU DON'T KEEP MOVING, YOU'LL FREEZE TO DEATH!!

WHAT'S WRONG, HYÔGA? STAND UP! STAND AND CONTINUE YOUR LESSON!!

UNH...

DON'T YOU WANT TO SEE YOUR MOTHER AGAIN?

HYÔGA, IF YOU SLEEP, YOU'LL DIE!

UNH...

144

REMEMBER, THOUGH SWANS FLOAT SERENELY UPON SIBERIA'S FRIGID SEAS, THEIR FEET PADDLE FRANTICALLY BELOW THE SURFACE!

IF YOU WANT TO HAVE THE SUPERHUMAN POWERS OF A KNIGHT, YOU MUST ENDURE SUFFERING BEYOND IMAGINATION!

HYÔGA!

WAKE UP, HYÔGA!!

GET UP!

WAKE UP, HYÔGA!!

HYÔGA!!

THE FROZEN AIR SWIRLING BETWEEN US WILL BLAST YOU TO PIECES!

HYÔGA!

HYÔGA!

THE FROZEN AIR IS ABOUT TO STRIKE YOU!!

HYÔGA! WAKE UP AND DODGE IT!

HAH!

OPEN YOUR EYES, HYÔGA!!

FWASH

HYÔGA!!

AGH!

WHAT!?

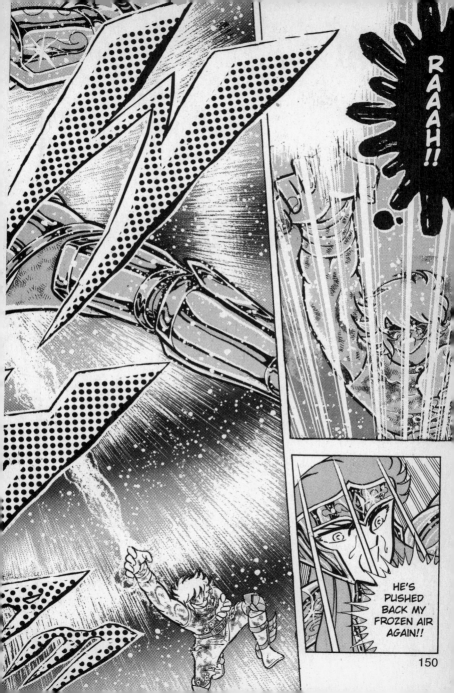

RAAAH!!

HE'S PUSHED BACK MY FROZEN AIR AGAIN!!

150

UGH!

WHA...

IT'S...

151

KR

MY GOLD CLOTH IS FROZEN!!

HIS FROZEN AIR HAD TO BE -459 DEGREES F...

IN ORDER TO SMASH THE FREEZING COFFIN, HE HAD TO PRODUCE FROZEN AIR COLDER THAN MY OWN!

BUT WHAT I SAID BEFORE HOLDS TRUE.

...ABSOLUTE ZERO!!

NEITHER YOUR FROZEN TORNADO NOR YOUR DIAMOND DUST HAD ANY EFFECT, AND YOU STAND HELPLESS BEFORE ME.

BUT NOW YOU'VE SURELY EXHAUSTED YOUR COSMO.

NOW I WILL BURY YOU...

YOUR DOOM WAS SEALED THE MOMENT YOU DARED TO FACE ME IN BATTLE!

THE AURORA EXECUTION!!

WHAT'S HE DOING!?

WH-WHAT!?

N-NO! CAN IT BE?

THE AURORA EXECUTION!!

IT'S HOPELESS! THE AURORA EXECUTION, AN IRRESISTIBLE BLAST OF FROZEN AIR, IS MY GREATEST MOVE!!

FOOL! NONE OF YOUR OWN MOVES WORKED, SO NOW YOU'D USE MY OWN MOVE AGAINST ME?

YOU MAY HAVE SURVIVED IT TWICE, BUT YOU WON'T MASTER IT SO EASILY!

YOU SHOULD KNOW THAT FROM FIRST-HAND EXPERIENCE!!

THE TRUE ESSENCE OF THE AURORA EXECUTION !!

TAKE THIS, HYÔGA!!

157

HYŌGA
IS NO
MORE...

A SINGLE
SNOWFLAKE...
AT THIS TIME
OF YEAR?

F
W
O
O
O

SHUN...

SEIYA!

SEIYA,
HYŌGA'S
COSMO JUST
SAID GOOD-
BYE TO US
...

WE DON'T
HAVE TIME
TO LOOK
BACK
ANYMORE...

DON'T
LOOK
BACK,
SHUN...

C'MON. IF WE CAN GET THROUGH THIS PALACE, THE MASTER'S CHAMBER LIES JUST BEYOND!

THE FINAL PALACE, THE PALACE OF THE TWIN FISH, IS JUST AHEAD!

WHAT?

SEIYA, WHEN WE ENTER THE PALACE, HEAD STRAIGHT FOR THE MASTER'S CHAMBER, NO MATTER WHAT HAPPENS.

R-RIGHT.

BUT... WHY?

ONE OF THE REASONS I FOUGHT MY WAY HERE WAS TO DEFEAT THE GOLD KNIGHT WHO GUARDS THE PALACE OF THE TWIN FISH.

LOOK OUT!!

UNH...

WELL DONE, HYÔGA.

HEH...

AND EVEN TEETERING BETWEEN LIFE AND FREEZING DEATH...

IN THIS BATTLE, WHILE ENDURING THE AURORA EXECUTION, YOU MANAGED TO MAKE IT YOUR OWN.

...WITH YOUR SENSES COMPLETELY GONE, YOU STILL MASTERED ABSOLUTE ZERO.

YOUR COSMO HAS FAR SURPASSED EVEN THAT OF YOUR TEACHER...

YOU HAVE LEARNED ALL I HAVE TO TEACH.

164

YOU HAVE AWAKENED THE VERY ESSENCE OF YOUR COSMO, THE SEVENTH SENSE!!

I WISH YOU A LONG LIFE.

IT IS MY HOPE THAT YOU WILL USE THAT POWER FOR A WORTHY CAUSE.

FORGIVE ME, HYŌGA...

...CAN DO NOTHING MORE FOR YOU!...

NOW IT SEEMS THAT EVEN I...

I'LL NEVER FORGET THE MANY THINGS YOU TAUGHT ME, CAMUS.

SOMEDAY... SOMEDAY, ONCE MORE...

...LET US RETURN TO THE FROZEN WASTES OF EASTERN SIBERIA TOGETHER...

THANK YOU, MASTER CAMUS...

...AND FAREWELL!!

167

CRIMSON ROSES?

WHO THREW THEM?

UNH!

168

HE KILLED THE MAN WHO TRAINED ME TO BE A KNIGHT ON ANDROMEDA ISLAND.

WHAT?

IT MUST'VE BEEN HIM...

SEIYA, THAT'S THE MAN I CAME HERE TO TAKE DOWN. WHATEVER HAPPENS, PLEASE DON'T INTERFERE.

SHUN!

I SWORE I'D AVENGE MY MASTER PERSONALLY.

...THE KNIGHT WHOSE BEAUTY IS SAID TO BE THE GREATEST OF THE 88 KNIGHTS...

THIS IS THE KNIGHT WHO GUARDS THE LAST OF THE 12 PALACES, THE PALACE OF THE TWIN FISH...

THE
BEAUTIFUL
WARRIOR
WHO SHINES
IN GLORY
BETWEEN
THE
HEAVENS
AND
EARTH!

TO BE CONTINUED IN VOLUME 12!

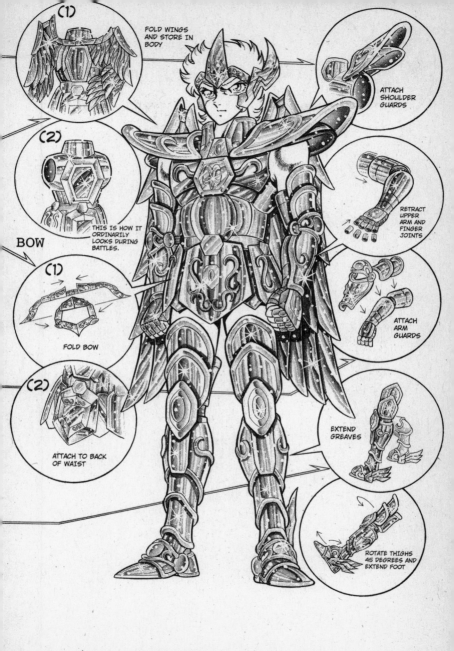

(1) FOLD WINGS AND STORE IN BODY

ATTACH SHOULDER GUARDS

(2) THIS IS HOW IT ORDINARILY LOOKS DURING BATTLES.

RETRACT UPPER ARM AND FINGER JOINTS

BOW

(1) FOLD BOW

ATTACH ARM GUARDS

(2) ATTACH TO BACK OF WAIST

EXTEND GREAVES

ROTATE THIGHS 45 DEGREES AND EXTEND FOOT

CLOTH BREAKDOWN AND FITTING CHART XXXVII

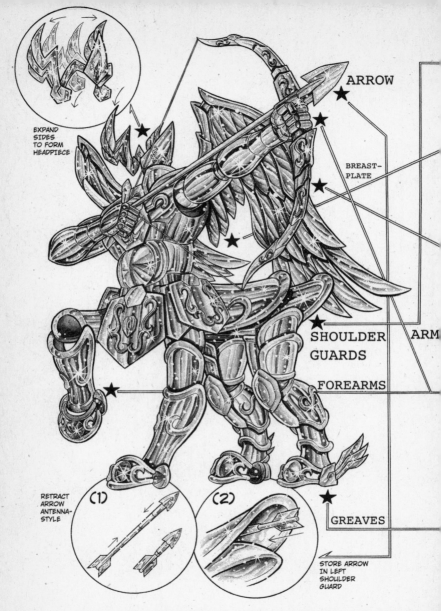

EXPAND
SIDES
TO FORM
HEADPIECE

ARROW

BREAST-
PLATE

ARM

SHOULDER
GUARDS

FOREARMS

RETRACT
ARROW
ANTENNA-
STYLE

(1)

(2)

STORE ARROW
IN LEFT
SHOULDER
GUARD

GREAVES

GOLD CLOTH BREAKDOWN AND FITTING CHART 9

THE SAGITTARIUS CLOTH

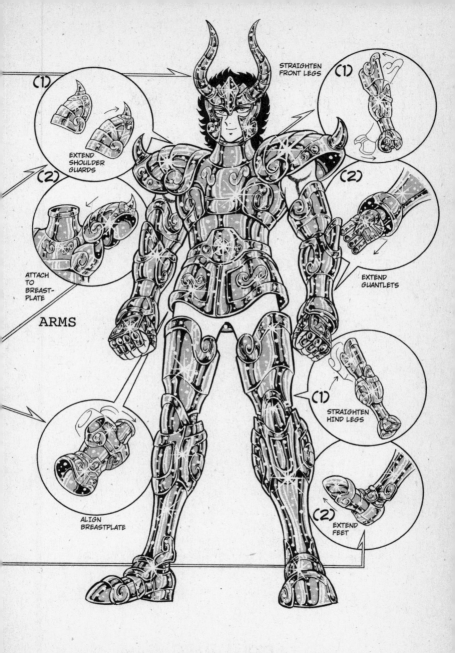

STRAIGHTEN
FRONT LEGS

(1)

(1)

EXTEND
SHOULDER
GUARDS

(2)

(2)

ATTACH
TO
BREAST-
PLATE

EXTEND
GUANTLETS

ARMS

(1)

STRAIGHTEN
HIND LEGS

ALIGN
BREASTPLATE

(2)

EXTEND
FEET

CLOTH BREAKDOWN AND FITTING CHART XXXVIII

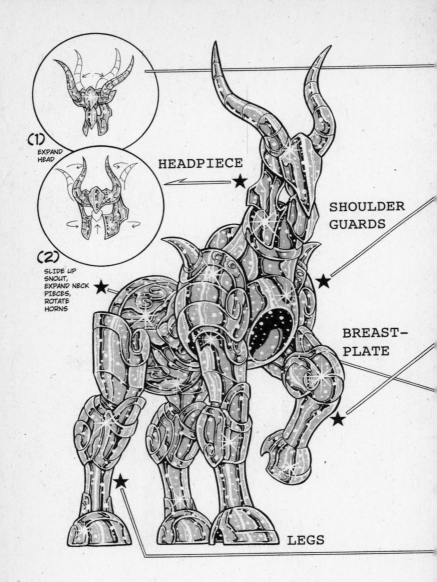

(1)
EXPAND
HEAD

(2)
SLIDE UP
SNOUT,
EXPAND NECK
PIECES,
ROTATE
HORNS

HEADPIECE ★

SHOULDER
GUARDS

BREAST-
PLATE

★

LEGS

GOLD CLOTH BREAKDOWN AND FITTING CHART 10

THE CAPRICORN CLOTH

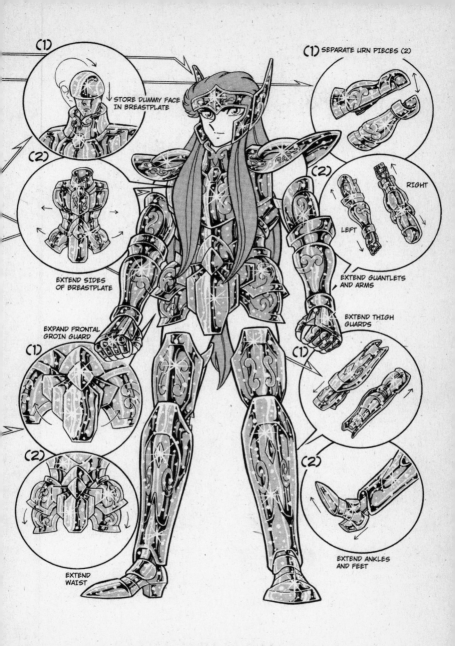

(1) ↓ STORE DUMMY FACE IN BREASTPLATE

(1) SEPARATE URN PIECES (2)

(2) EXTEND SIDES OF BREASTPLATE

(2) LEFT RIGHT

EXTEND GUANTLETS AND ARMS

EXPAND FRONTAL GROIN GUARD

(1)

EXTEND THIGH GUARDS

(1)

(2) EXTEND WAIST

(2)

EXTEND ANKLES AND FEET

CLOTH BREAKDOWN AND FITTING CHART XXXIX

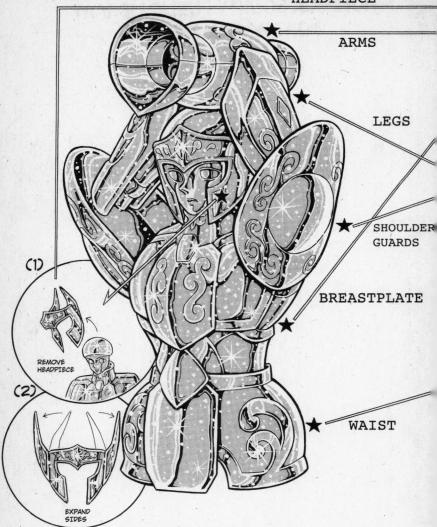

HEADPIECE

ARMS

LEGS

SHOULDER
GUARDS

BREASTPLATE

WAIST

(1)

REMOVE
HEADPIECE

(2)

EXPAND
SIDES

GOLD CLOTH BREAKDOWN AND FITTING CHART 11

THE AQUARIUS CLOTH

COMING NEXT VOLUME:

Only one Gold Knight stands between the Bronze Knights
and the Master of Sanctuary: Aphrodite, the Pisces Knight.
Shun volunteers to fight Aphrodite alone, to avenge his
teacher's death…but soon both Seiya and Shun are paralyzed
by Aphrodite's Demon Rose attacks! Beyond Aphrodite's
palace waits the mysterious Master of Sanctuary. But who is
the Master…and does he really have the power to save
Princess Sienna?

AVAILABLE IN NOVEMBER 2005!

COMPLETE OUR SURVEY AND LET US KNOW WHAT YOU THINK!

☐ Please do NOT send me information about VIZ and SHONEN JUMP products, news and events, special offers, or other information.

☐ Please do NOT send me information from VIZ's trusted business partners.

Name: _____

Address: _____

City: _____ **State:** _____ **Zip:** _____

E-mail: _____

☐ **Male** ☐ **Female**   **Date of Birth (mm/dd/yyyy):** ___/___/_____   (Under 13? Parental consent required)

❶ **Do you purchase SHONEN JUMP Magazine?**

☐ Yes   ☐ No (if no, skip the next two questions)

If **YES**, do you subscribe?
☐ Yes   ☐ No

If **NO**, how often do you purchase SHONEN JUMP Magazine?

☐ 1-3 issues a year

☐ 4-6 issues a year

☐ more than 7 issues a year

❷ **Which SHONEN JUMP Graphic Novel did you purchase? (please check one)**

☐ Beet the Vandel Buster   ☐ Bleach   ☐ Dragon Ball
☐ Dragon Ball Z   ☐ Dr. Slump   ☐ Eyeshield 21
☐ Hikaru no Go   ☐ Hunter x Hunter   ☐ I"s
☐ Knights of the Zodiac   ☐ Legendz   ☐ Naruto
☐ One Piece   ☐ Rurouni Kenshin   ☐ Shaman King
☐ The Prince of Tennis   ☐ Ultimate Muscle   ☐ Whistle!
☐ Yu-Gi-Oh!   ☐ Yu-Gi-Oh!: Duelist   ☐ YuYu Hakusho
☐ Other _____

Will you purchase subsequent volumes?
☐ Yes   ☐ No

❸ **How did you learn about this title? (check all that apply)**

☐ Favorite title   ☐ Advertisement   ☐ Article
☐ Gift   ☐ Read excerpt in SHONEN JUMP Magazine
☐ Recommendation   ☐ Special offer   ☐ Through TV animation
☐ Website   ☐ Other _____

4 Of the titles that are serialized in SHONEN JUMP Magazine, have you purchased the Graphic Novels?

☐ Yes ☐ No

If **YES**, which ones have you purchased? (check all that apply)

☐ Dragon Ball Z ☑ Hikaru no Go ☑ Naruto ☑ One Piece
☐ Shaman King ☐ Yu-Gi-Oh! ☐ YuYu Hakusho

If **YES**, what were your reasons for purchasing? (please pick up to 3)

☐ A favorite title ☐ A favorite creator/artist ☐ I want to read it in one go
☐ I want to read it over and over again ☐ There are extras that aren't in the magazine
☐ The quality of printing is better than the magazine ☐ Recommendation
☐ Special offer ☐ Other

If **NO**, why did/would you not purchase it?

☐ I'm happy just reading it in the magazine ☐ It's not worth buying the graphic novel
☐ All the manga pages are in black and white unlike the magazine
☐ There are other graphic novels that I prefer ☐ There are too many to collect for each title
☐ It's too small ☐ Other _____

5 Of the titles NOT serialized in the Magazine, which ones have you purchased?
(check all that apply)

☐ Beet the Vandel Buster ☐ Bleach ☐ Dragon Ball ☐ Dr. Slump
☐ Eyeshield 21 ☐ Hunter x Hunter ☐ I"s ☐ Knights of the Zodiac
☐ Legendz ☐ The Prince of Tennis ☐ Rurouni Kenshin ☐ Whistle!
☐ Yu-Gi-Oh!: Duelist ☐ None ☐ Other _____

If you did purchase any of the above, what were your reasons for purchase?

☐ A favorite title ☐ A favorite creator/artist
☐ Read a preview in SHONEN JUMP Magazine and wanted to read the rest of the story
☐ Recommendation ☐ Other

Will you purchase subsequent volumes?

☐ Yes ☐ No

6 What race/ethnicity do you consider yourself? (please check one)

☐ Asian/Pacific Islander ☐ Black/African American ☐ Hispanic/Latino
☐ Native American/Alaskan Native ☐ White/Caucasian ☐ Other

THANK YOU! Please send the completed form to: VIZ Survey
42 Catharine St.
Poughkeepsie, NY 12601

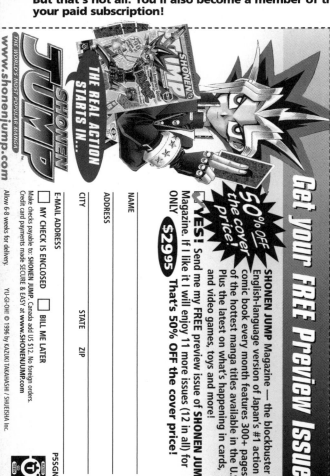

Check us out
on the web!

www.shonenjump.com

BUSINESS REPLY MAIL
FIRST-CLASS MAIL   PERMIT NO. 113   MT MORRIS IL

POSTAGE WILL BE PAID BY ADDRESSEE

NO POSTAGE
NECESSARY
IF MAILED
IN THE
UNITED STATES

SUBSCRIPTIONS SERVICE DEPT.
PO BOX 509
MT. MORRIS IL 61054-7763

S0-BAL-950